Questions About Home

Questions About Home ©2014 Cynthia Brackett-Vincent
Author photograph © Dory Diaz

ISBN-10: 1-893035-21-2
ISBN-13: 978-1-893035-21-8

All rights reserved. No part of this book may be reproduced in any form by any mechanical or electronic means including storage and retrieval systems without express permission in writing from the publisher. Brief passages may be quoted in review.

Editor: Devin McGuire

Book design and cover design: Eddie Vincent/ENC Graphics Services

Cover photograph ©2011 Cynthia Brackett-Vincent

Questions About Home

poems by
Cynthia Brackett-Vincent

Encircle Publications, LLC
Farmington, Maine

*Grateful acknowledgement is made to the editors
of the following print and online publications
in which these poems appeared (some in slightly different versions):*

"All the Hungry Animals," *Stanza* (Maine Poets Society);
"Come Morning," *Pirene's Fountain*; *First Water: Best of Pirene's Fountain* (Glass Lyre Press, 2012);
"How Much Work to Hum Those Wings," *Maine Taproot: An Anthology of Verse* (Maine Poets Society, 2010);
"Hummingbirds Instead," *Pirene's Fountain*; *First Water: Best of Pirene's Fountain*;
"If One Felt In Need," *Forever Friends* (Mandinam Press, 2008);
"In Maine," *Yankee*;
"It's just me & a fingernail moon," *Mannequin Envy*;
"Just two weekends ago I was thinking," *Pirene's Fountain*;
"Leaning on a gravestone," *Mannequin Envy*;
"Maine, Orion," *Harbor Journal*; *Pirene's Fountain*;
"North, After Freeport," *Maine Taproot: An Anthology of Verse*;
"Poetry," *Decanto*;
"The Rhythm of Her Hymns," *Orange Room Review*;
"Stolen Pears," *And Still I Return to Love: Remembering Russell Libby* (2012); *Pandora's Box* (Inkception Books, 2013);
"Valentine's Day Blizzard," *The Anthology of New England Writers 2008*;
"When Even the Inanimate Seems to Rise & Fall With Breath," *Yankee*.

In addition:

"Kodi Ball," *the Aurorean; Favorites from the First Fifteen Years* (Encircle Publications, 2012);
"This Is My Maine," *the Aurorean*.

*The author expresses heartfelt appreciation to
Devin McGuire—friend and colleague—for his careful editing.*

Poems

I.

This Is My Maine 3

Maine, Orion 4

Just two weekends ago I was thinking 5

How Much Work to Hum Those Wings 6

Valentine's Day Blizzard 7

Mid-February, treetops 8

When Even the Inanimate Seems to Rise & Fall With Breath 9

Hummingbirds Instead 10

Sacred Thanks 11

Come Morning 12

It's just me & a fingernail moon 13

All the Hungry Animals 14

Rainy Day—I imagine 15

In Maine, ...16

My friend talks of her *beloved cardinal* 17

North, After Freeport 18

The Rhythm of Her Hymns 19

Tanka for Poseidon 20

How to Love a Cat 21

Kodi 22

Kodi Ball 23

My husband drives our midnight-blue Jeep at dusk 24

Questions About Home 25

II.

In the black of night as if 29
How it Was That He Laughed Still 30
To Feed My Father 31
Father's Day 32
If only, I could imagine them always 33
Our Duplicity 34
Leaning on a gravestone, ...36
Goodbye to College at Forty-Seven 37
Hymn of Praise 38
If One Felt in Need 39
Early-Arrived Angel 40
Waiting for Olivia 41
After the Adoption Ceremony 42
Youngest Son of My Youngest Son 43
In the MRI Tube I 44
In the MRI Tube II 45
Winter Lost 46
These Perfect Days 47
To Live So Lustily 48
Some Days 49
Poet Laureate 50
Poetry 51
Princess Diana is Dead & Fun Town Has Closed. 52
Stolen Pears 53

About the Author 55

to Eddie & Lisa

I.

This Is My Maine

On a soundless Sunday morning—
save for second hands on two clocks
each ticking its own imperfect time—
we wake to first, fresh snow;
it will vanish by noon.

But for now my husband looks up
from reading his *Discover*,
props his chin up with his wrist,
tries to see what I see
through the window,
over the woods sprinkled white.

My father on his wedding day
in a photo on the wall
looks out, too,
over the trees he would have carefully measured,
called by name. He'd like to be
climbing them, pruning them,
counting rings of the less fortunate,
splinters no matter.

This one moment in time is my Maine,
this November 21 a.m.
Its very seconds will be ticked away;
its little flakes melt point by point,
but here it is now, solid as the oak
whose branch brushes my crystal-gleaming pane.

Maine, Orion

Unforgiving November sky here.
Orion ascends over dark fingers of trees.

I remember how my father pronounced *Betelgeuse*—
bright star of the Hunter's shoulder—
how he pointed with his big toe,
arms limp with polio but strong left leg lifted high,
cut-outs scissored into the tips of each sock.

I remember when my son first traced
the flashing belt, the pointed sword—
raising his little mitten up, up—
into all the galaxies
born that night on the salty air.

Arms reach to draw me into drowsy
sleep. Betelgeuse blinks. *Somewhere, father.*

Just two weekends ago I was thinking

how we didn't work on our landscape plans this year,
how all these years we've been saying
what we will do. How that one last
mowing, raking, picking up the yard got away,
how our neighbor's land is perfect, even fieldstones in their place.

But today I think how winter equals us all in Maine—
eighteen inches of snow, my path pristine as theirs—
us out in the driveway of our mobile home with shovels,
them down the road with theirs. How we're all supposed
to dig out mailboxes by eight in the morning,
each of us somehow comforted to hear the other
scraping the ground.

How Much Work to Hum Those Wings

Such a small thing
to catch my eye—
pale green patch of lichen
against gray sky.
Seems far away
from the path I carve out
as I shovel,
far away from summer
when the hummingbird
came. Always on that high branch,
always on that fuzzy
bit of haven, bit of rest.
How much work to hum
those wings! How much work
to raise up another mound of snow.

Valentine's Day Blizzard

The snow we've wished for all winter has come.
Has come in whipped-up wind stinging my face
as we dig out the mailbox & shovel
the roof. We make games of it—when the gusts
bring tears, I say he looks like his brother,
laughing as the sun glints off his glasses
when he realizes his truck plow is stuck.
We start at ends & meet in the middle;

a mouse skitters across a drift. We fall
into bed later, too tired for love
but for bars of bittersweet chocolate
we pass back & forth between us—their foil
heaped around us like the clothes of our youth,
silver, shiny, as each last bit of ice.

Mid-February, treetops

seem tinged with buds.
Most every tree, reddish buds.

High up, only a jet's white
contrails dissolving.

Dead trees still reaching up
for glint of ice, another's leaf on wind.

Impressions my neighbor's cat made in the night—
pads of paws now thinly set in snow.

When Even the Inanimate Seems to Rise & Fall With Breath

It's that time of year in Maine—
same time six years ago
when together we fell in love with this bit of rocky land
after one traipse around its woodsy path,
one round trip down the gravel road—
that godly time in May in Maine when even
the inanimate seems to rise & fall with breath—
when along the road fiddleheads still knot tightly into fists,
the grading truck now come & gone—when you can hit fifty
in the Jeep, when everything
but this one moment & your future
billow out behind you in a cloud of dust.

Hummingbirds Instead

Inbox full, but I'm outside
chasing hummingbirds instead—
camera bouncing back & forth
each time they flit from tree to tree.
On the next bough & then the next—
needle-beak silhouette dark against sky
ruby-flash quick on blue
& suddenly I see the rest—as if my indoor eyes
had fallen away—
buttercups tall, sun-creamy yellow
& the blackberries—blackberries flowering
white like lace—
like love.

Sacred Thanks

—for Emma & John

As the earth sighs slightly toward autumn's colder constellations,
the last of my neighbors' summer squash stand like ancient symbols
in my kitchen. The two lean against each other, losing their fullness.

Overflowing bags found each morning on the lip
of my mailbox—now, a half-dozen cherry tomatoes remain
in a peach-colored bowl. Each time I walk by they seem to ask
what exactly it is I am waiting for.

For tonight, I say. For Orion to sheath his great sword,
for the sunflowers to bow their magnificent heads,
for me to give proper thanks.

Come Morning

> *Now faith is the substance of things hoped for,*
> *the evidence of things not seen.*
> —Hebrews 11:1, KJV

September's early dusk. Kaleidoscope of light
through low trees. Starbursts become pinholes,
play tricks on the eyes. Minute by minute
each disappears. My small corner of earth gives up day.
What was there—perhaps there now—reduced
to faulty memory. Suspect memory. Nothing
to hold onto. Lights to turn on in here.

Yet this is the time the deer will come. A doe
with her fawn. In a precarious thicket between
summer & fall, she'll teach him to nuzzle
only the choicest gems—cones dark as moonless night,
seedy & oversweet. I know this. Come morning,
dew-covered & new-sunlit fruits will gleam
on the ground. Come morning, the grasses will genuflect.

It's just me & a fingernail moon

walking my neighbor's letters down the dirt road
to her mailbox where they belong
when suddenly I realize it *is* just us
me, the moon, & the old stone wall
which leans in a little closer, it seems
each year to the roadside's curve
a little bit like love, a little bit like need
while my hip screams louder
with each nuance of gravel
each boot-plod up the hill—
distance between neighbors
so close, so far. But we get there,
just me & the scurrying squirrels
intent on filling up, me
the red squirrels
the old stone wall
fingernail moon at our backs now
& the wind helping us home—
just us & as good a day
as we all may get.

All the Hungry Animals

Eleven o'clock at night & I think about what my friend said over lunch,
how she's never been to Wal-Mart, how she hopes
in this small way to change the world.

But here I am tooling off to that Great Beacon of Light Pollution
20 miles away, because when I went to do that one last thing before bed
I discovered it was dog food I bought for my cats, earlier, in haste.

What am I supposed to do smack in middle of Maine—
General Store locked up tight hours ago, while its owners already dream
in their upstairs beds. So it's just me & all the other hungry animals on the road—
dust kicking up around us, their eyes catching in the headlights of my Jeep along the way.

Rainy day—I imagine

my friends seated in a semi-circle
on my lawn—backs to the house,
faces toward woods. Ice cubes clink
as lemonade is raised, sipped, swirled.
Their words are like those of ghosts—
hushed, jumbled. Or in that pitch
only angels & animals can hear.

Phrases begin to drift in,
fall on my ears—
talk of daisies, Black-Eyed Susans,
Queen Anne's Lace. It seems as if every flower
is accounted for as it bends to the wind.
I hear as if for the first time
words like *quiver, floret, dragonfly, wing.*

In Maine,

virgin soil becomes tilled; oxen strain
to pull a large fieldstone from its place.
The hard crack is heard of stone on stone—
each one upon the last as walls are built up.
Women in long dresses bend, pluck blackberries
from the sun. Inside, precious crimson syrup
seeps through sieves.

Now drumbeats hush as arrowheads whoosh
through air. Long strips of birch bark
are peeled from trees, fastened into homes.
Along the Sandy River, the Amaseconti—
First Ones Here.

Even this ledge-rock
once trembled against ice. In its striations,
the teeth of a glacier live. My fingers
caress what became smooth from the rough.

      My father's voice echoes in the fallen tree's rings.
          Each ring is a year:
            In each ring—
                listen!—the story of a year.

My friend talks of her *beloved cardinal*

—for Judy

how the Sharp-shinned Hawk swooped in
how in a blink the strong & the fragile were one

how she so wanted to hate that hawk
but asks, *How could I begrudge him his survival?*

Of the female at the feeder for days, hunger
unyielding—unwilling to eat even a bit of seed.

Then the part I least expected—how a new flicker of red—
bold as sunrise—alit & began to feed.

North, After Freeport

Another hour I'll be home
but for now, seems we're all flying North

some of us bumper-hugging
others lagging behind in the rear view

a few ahead with taillights fading
like sunsets we long to pursue.

Unlikely chain of travelers—
truckers, poets, lost souls

hurtling forward
into charcoal clouds of dusk.

Half-moon, first stars & fireflies
going somewhere too

as we zoom over darkened ribbons
of the Androscoggin, the Cobboseecontee.

Nothing else seems to matter—
our ones stacked together in the toll takers' drawers.

The Rhythm of Her Hymns

Some keep the Sabbath going to Church—
—Emily Dickinson

Sunday morning, Medusa on my lap,
my fingers warm in her white belly fur.
Her purrs—soft chants
as golden bits of October heaven
fall to earth. Church is starting soon.
Outside, a jet's contrails form
a steeple in the crisp-clean sky.
Medusa touches my hand with hers,
the pads of her paws warm.
I close my eyes, listen to the rhythm of her hymns,
devotion enough for both of us.

Tanka for Poseidon

Fingers stroking fur—
do plains lions purr like this?
His mouth slack, small teeth
like needles against my palm.
No hyenas in these dreams.

How to Love a Cat

—for Panoptes

See into the shelter's cages. Into the cats' eyes. Watch one
as it watches you walk by. Go back to that one,
insert a finger into a rectangular hole. Then, think
of the tiny space in which this would-be companion
ekes out a life. As if you lived in your tiniest closet.

A closet of steel. Although you notice all that goes on,
most of what goes on goes on without noticing you.
Sometimes, your door slides open, so that on a good day
you are let out to stretch your legs. After a time, you are put back.
Workers predictably fill up your bowls. Next to your food,
you must perform your most private functions. Occasionally, a shiny toy
is thrown your way. If you play with it, you must do so in solitude.

But you are not in a steel closet; you are at the shelter looking in.
One is looking out. At you. I could tell you he won't be much trouble,
but that may or may not be true. I could tell you he won't swat you,
refuse your litter box, claw up your couch. But once you call him by name,
there is no going back, no sliding his steel door back down between you,
no walking out of the shelter door catless, no falling asleep
without warm belly fur to rub.

Kodi

—November 1999–August 2009

No matter his back leg that drags,
nor the infection just opened up again,
he whines to go, climbs into my husband's truck

as if it's any other day, as if the two are only setting out
on their daily ritual. Post Office, grocery, pizza pick-up dog.
Tongue-hanging, tail-wagging, errand-companion dog.

It is the trust that gets to me—the trust
that could lead him anywhere. For instance, now—
his silly dog-smile as the silver Ford propels him away.

Kodi Ball

Lodged under a log—itself now rooting back to ground—
early snowmelt unearths the bright pink & green tennis ball.

A Kodi ball. I think, *That's all he needed*, consider digging out the ball,
placing it near his ashes in the stone wall. But it's still too cold to move fieldstone.

All he needed: A ball, a shiny bowl of water, food whenever we put it down.
The chance to protect us while we walked the woods. While in our sleep.

When we sat down, how he sat, too, sighing as his weight gave in,
his not-so-old Shepherd bones losing texture bit by bit—like snow.

My husband drives our midnight-blue Jeep at dusk

on Route 3. Lights shimmer ahead in the Pru, the Hancock.
The Pine Street Inn watches us go by. We head down into the O'Neal
& I think of my uncle driving me north for holidays—
his smile, him telling me to duck down as we went into the tunnel.

Eddie lane-jumps a quick-left before we emerge, straight-shot
onto the Zakim. Centrifugal force swings us around the arc
toward the shaky Tobin. The old green hunchback propels us as we descend—
head-start onto Route 1. I try to look into the windows of Chelsea, Revere,
but can't hold any in view along this concrete corridor. Soon it's all stores,
strip clubs, gas stations, donut shops, malls, motels.
At 95 North he blinks a right. We pass the exit to my mother's cemetery,
my uncle's house. The ghosts of Danvers State Hospital play in the near-dark
on the hill. I lay back the seat at the 39 miles to Portsmouth sign.
Route 1 keeps whooshing in my head.

I feel the Jeep slow; the cold air swirls in when his window goes down.
He mumbles a thank you at the Hampton tolls—Maine border so close now,
I wait, eyes closed, until the Piscataqua takes us up, over, down,
leaves our old lives south in the night wind. Next thing I know,
we're over the Androscoggin, over the Cobbosseecontee—those silvery watery veins
in Maine's dark night. I remind him to watch out for deer, for moose. An hour later
it's the familiar frostheaves of our dirt road. I scooch up in my seat
to find four stars in our headlights—two young deer.
The pair walks the road ahead of us like guides—
too small to jump the late-March snowbanks. First chance they get, they bolt.
Inside, our cats rub up against our legs as if to say
Don't leave us again.

Questions About Home

When are you moving home?, I am asked.
In turn I say, *Have you heard the loon call?*
Have you seen scrape-marks of a glacier's teeth?
Cars whiz by their homes, their kids. Lightning speed.

In turn I say, *Have you heard the loon call?*
Is where you're from necessarily home?
Cars whiz by their homes, their kids. Lightning speed.
Blackberries ripen. We watch, wait for deer.

Is where you're from necessarily home?
Home is where your soul finally sees it.
Blackberries ripen. We watch, wait for deer.
Why Maine? What on earth made you move there?

Home is where your soul finally sees it.
I saw the woods like my father showed me.
Why Maine? What on earth made you move there?
The luminescent stars, calling us home.

II.

In the black of night as if

the whole world exploded at once,
a green truck lies upside-down,
tires spinning, sparks like meteors
tracing themselves to earth
as electric wires sway in the dark.

We have come outside to Armageddon.
My husband's bare feet
drip with blood from tiny pieces
of glass—the windshield through which
moments ago, four boys fixed their eyes
brightly ahead.

One is face-down on my lawn.
I think to go to him. He is too still.
His gray sweatshirt softly covers his head.
I pray for him as if he is one of my sons
dead. As rescue vehicles finally arrive—
too late—his gold chain shimmers in the light,
shimmers between blades of grass.

How it Was That He Laughed Still

His stories, his father's stories—
how he loved each
more & more with each telling.
How polio offered my father the luxury
of rumination, as my sister & I sat—one
at his side—one at the foot
of his bed. How he laughed in the incomplete way
being paralyzed allowed. Sometimes
I'd stare at the ring embossed into the skin
of his thin neck, reminder of two years
in an iron lung. I'd wonder how
it was that he laughed still, how he wanted
to tell us stories each night, while our mother
only swept around us now in wide circles,
calling from the distant kitchen
when supper was done.

To Feed My Father

—Carlton Brackett: June 14, 1928–December 22, 1999

I'm already halfway in, pushing
myself through my father's doorway,
sweaty brass knob in hand
when I remember to roll up
the cotton socks I'd only wear
to his house on such a stifling day,
cover Sagittarius' bold red arrow
tattooed on my left ankle—
pagan symbol to this faithful man of God
who waits sleeping. Waits
for his daughter, for his dinner, for December.

Father's Day

> *Some keep the Sabbath going to Church—*
> *I keep it, staying at Home—*
> *With a Bobolink for a Chorister—*
> *And an Orchard, for a Dome—*
> —Emily Dickinson

Were he to tell the story,
 I didn't do so well
those last years he was here—
left the house in which he worshiped,
& like Emily, stayed home.

But what if today
were before that bitter time?
I'd honor him
with one of his famous weather experiments—
or with a sturdy jar of glass
let him show me how quickly
cola rots a tooth.

I'd follow his directions carefully,
stand side by side. Father, daughter,
earning separate spots in heaven
by doing what we do.

If only, I could imagine them always

this way: my father, perched high on the roof,
sun-down at his back. Coffee steams
from an open Thermos—his attention
for the briefest moment each evening
lost on a young woman with black hair
& her red plaid coat as it tosses in the wind
when she leaves through the Salem factory gate.
This, the good morning of the watchman's nights.

Our Duplicity

My better self carries saltines
& small plastic cups
of ginger-ale into the rooms
of the elderly. I sit,
put all 17 years & 99 pounds of me
into brushing long gray strands
of Eunice's hair. She calls me
Sunshine, not Cindy.
She has had someone
tape my wedding announcement
to her oak mirror—
the one thing
the nursing home allowed her to bring
from home. Everyone who enters her room
must read the newspaper clipping
at Eunice's insistence.

    Now I carry saltines
& a can of ginger-ale
into Aunt Sarah's room
after she banishes the kitchen aide—
I can't eat that!
she screamed. I wonder
at the aide's lack of interest
in a patient's eating at all
as he offered up nothing else.
But I'm used to Sarah—
Sergeant Sarah, United States Army, WWII.
She tells me I should have been a nurse
as I open the crackers,
snap the tab on the can.
I tell her how easy it was

to walk in the staff kitchen,
how they always stock Jello & soda,
even bread for toast.
Her stern face softens a bit
as she considers our duplicity.
Like bits of stars, little crumbs fall from her mouth.

Leaning on a gravestone,

my sister waits for me above the bones of ancestors—
Wilkins, Crofts, Hutchinsons. When I arrive
we sip coffee near our mother's stone, talk of how
she'd have liked a Hazelnut—iced—how the ground
will be newly turned here soon; of the need for flowers
as our last Aunt lies dying. We wonder how it will be
for Uncle Dave—all his siblings gone. What we think,
but do not say, is that one of us will know someday—
perched above some stony symbol of a life—here,
alone.

Good-Bye to College at Forty-Seven

—after "Goodbye to the Old Life" by Wesley McNair

Good-bye to the red-haired cafeteria lady,
Kathy, whose name—my sister's—
made me feel at home;

good-bye to the one ladies room,
ice-cold water winter & summer
with which to punish one's hands clean;

good-bye to the patches of yellow daffodils,
which, through Yankee persistence
turn up spring after spring;

good-bye to the unilluminated pathways
behind the Student Center—
treacherous on Maine's early-dark nights;

    & as for this sunny May a.m. with its tassels—
hung this way then that—even to you—your caps
airborne in youth's palpable joy,

    you with parents cheering, me with grown sons!—
    yes!—here's to you & me:
Good-bye to college as we commence with life.

Hymn of Praise

My daughter-in-law sings,
"Mr. Noah, would you like
 a crib by the window this evening?"

"Mr. Noah, would you like pears
with your oatmeal? Cream on the side?"
Noah smiles back at her

with complete abandon,
& I catch a glint of morning light
shining in my son's eyes as he watches,

these two—his two—how this woman he loves
sings her morning hymn, how the son he loves
holds the universe with one breath.

If One Felt in Need

It's the kind of thing one might get comfort from
if one felt in need of it—let's say on a late-March
Maine afternoon—just knowing that these two women
love your sons. That while you sip tea in bed
they are in Massachusetts having theirs, brainstorming
a business plan, the next birthday,
or dinner next time you're home. That one listens
intently for your grandson, that both
wait to wrap their arms around him when he wakes.
That the roles have so gently turned in this life,
that you can fall asleep now, dream of rocking your sons.

Early-Arrived Angel

—for Ashlyn

You can't even think of what you should pack,
but you throw things in a suitcase
just the same. One pair of socks—or ten?

You hate yourself for the time it takes
to figure out the away message on your computer,
for grabbing binders, papers, work-in-progress. Still

you have no clothes packed to speak of, only socks.
You think a cigarette might help
but you might not even know your name if asked.

Your son & daughter-in-law sit in neonatal
intensive care as their early-arrived angel struggles
with earth-air—tiny CPAP machine easing the transition

from womb to world. Your trip
from Maine to Boston seems slow-motioned,
backward. Hawks watch from the roadside
as you hurtle along.

All that time—all that distance—
becomes irrelevant
when she is gently placed in your arms.

Waiting for Olivia

—for Maria

What I most remember
isn't the curl of black hair I saw crowning
first, or the midwife's face

nor those hours in the lobby—
automatic door opening, shutting,
opening to January chill—

as I waited for my son
to tell me it was time. Images
of a warming bed, emergency equipment

just in case. The clock on the wall, plain-faced.
Nathan holding Lucy; Lucy's mother & me clenched hand in hand—
fingernails digging in deeper with each contraction.

What I will most remember
is the prayer.
Lucy's mother's determined words

intoned in Portuguese—
none of it I understood but for *Amen*.
How her prayer was my prayer—everymother's.

After the Adoption Ceremony

Our new grandson asks to come with us.
Son & daughter-in-law help him climb in our Jeep.
He carries his new Teddy bear—a gift from the judge.

We bring him to lunch, let him order up what he wants—
There is picture-taking: *Say cheese!* All dressed up still,
we head to the waterfront. When we walk the jetty,
he runs ahead of us, moving along the harbor's stone barrier
like a puppy let loose. (I have seen this joy in my son.)

The tails of his blue shirt come untucked as he skips along in the wind.
We decide on ice cream next; I offer my hand, help him jump from the rocks.
One last photo, though: He sits & poses on a great anchor standing sentinel in sand.

Youngest Son of My Youngest Son

It never gets old, the phone call announcing
another grand, racing the Jeep from Maine
to Massachusetts to hold new life in your hands.

We as grandparents become born again.
Michael—archangel—his middle name.

This is life that came *through* me and *to* me.
Through ancestors, through all of the sons of earth—
all of the particles of universe in one—
This new son of my youngest son.

In the MRI Tube I

I imagine the technicians
will find bits of poems in there—
little dancing letters eluding them
in a labyrinth of gray matter—
the names of all my past loves
half-written, repeating themselves
in sestinas & villanelles,
long-gone loved ones' initials,
faded elegies & epitaphs.
My arms stiffen at my side
& I wish I could relax as only the dead
are allowed. The machine clicks its metallic noises
& when all goes silent, surely, I think,
they have come to what they are looking for—
the perfect title stops them—left to its devices,
the poem has been editing itself for years.

In the MRI Tube II

I think about what the technicians might see
as they inject colorful dye into my veins,
follow it along a rivery trail
to find what is wrong.

I imagine rainbows of color spreading,
blossoming, every rainbow I have ever seen
imprinted in a memory card deep
in my mind. I see

the double rainbow as it arched over
Mount Washington on that autumn day;
thick rainbows of oil in puddles
I played in as a child; the half-rainbow
not so long ago on Route 95,
so incomprehensible I had to stop right there
in the sun-dappled rain.

Perhaps Noah's rainbow, as he bumped along
to a halt on Ararat, cleared forty nights
of drowsiness from his eyes,
crept out of that sea-tossed ark
& into the palpable light.

Winter Lost

(to Lyme Disease & a foot fracture)

The mounded snow is a galaxy glinting with stars.
It is a thousand scarves draped over the stone wall.
Each whirl of the universe calls my name.
Each soft fold along the rough-laid rocks calls my name.

The stars are suns burning my skin.
The scarves warm only the rocks.
My snowshoes hang, metal teeth ready.
I drag my foot cast around the house.

I want to be the universe.
I want to wrap myself in hot snow.
Flaming-cold suns. Be out there.
Lie down on rocks, burn in the snow.

These Perfect Days

—after "The Life of a Day" by Tom Hennen

I've been in a funk for a long time (which is not a particularly poetic way
to begin a poem & I won't take these parentheses & ampersands out
even in the case the majority in my workshops object). But it's been poor me,
poor me, why me with this illness. I can't teach, can't hike, drive most of the time,
go outside all summer long—pick those blackberries just beyond my window,
be trusted not to drop a grandchild on his/her head. But these days have gone along
perfectly fine. The dog's company, the cats' company—unearthly sweet. Go-to-ness
of a husband, calls, visits, kids. Kids who bring with them those grandchildren—
who, in themselves are content with the day, each shiny thing within reach,
no matter their complete helplessness of which they are perfectly content
to remain unaware. So too this day will go along—cats will jump on my lap,
a slight breeze stir in my view, a doe feast on blackberries I would have hoarded
for myself. On the white table, the lemon-scented candle mesmerizes as it flickers,
softly collapsing in on itself.

To Live So Lustily

—after "For the Sleepwalkers" by Edward Hirsch

I'd like to draw your attention
to the dwindling fireflies of summer.
Years past, one particular night
a million million hatched,
outstretched their wings,
snap-snapping luminescence
rousing me out of sleep.
Now scientists are worried—
& I'm inspired by halves.

If I could say a brilliant thing
to call them back,
It might be as the scripture somewhat goes,

> *You are the light of the world!*
> *The fires in our hearts burn cooler now.*
> *Don't leave us in the darkness of June.*

I want to have their faith again—
even in the dark—to know
my bright brief time on earth will come—
to live so lustily as to light up all the world.

Some Days

Some days you just want to sit outside, smoke a cigarette & have iced coffee
with your mom. But you don't smoke & your mom has passed, so you sit
on the steps drinking blueberry tea, thinking about her. You're used to thinking
about her in all the old ways: how you always had to take care of her, how she
constantly yelled at your helpless dad. But the more you sit & think, the more
you remember little things she did. You want her to walk to your house & make
you cinnamon toast, take care of the boys, pour Downey into the washing machine.
She'd be at a loss about your diagnosis & all she'd be able to say would be
Don't' overdo it, now. But I'd overdo it. I'd take her out to lunch, slip a few dollars
into her purse, buy her & Daddy a lobster roll for supper, give her a ride back
to Phoenix Court, say how good the laundry smells now & thanks for her help.

Poet Laureate

—for Wes McNair

He never had a chance. Me running,
waving at him in the dark parking lot
like a crazed fan. Over landscaped mulch,
back onto pavement—closer, closer still.
I think he considers his escape routes.
Cynthia!, he realizes. Kiss on the cheek.
He & my husband tower over me.
We catch up. The fullest of moons looks on,
illuminates his head. He listens
as if his life depended on the listening.
This is what he meant those years ago in class:
Get down to the poem.
What is the poem trying to say?

Poetry

is in the low afternoon light
as it filters slowly through the pines. Somewhere
in the gray matter before you fall asleep.
It is lost in one of 10,000 words
you might have written down,
all those headlights already whooshed by.
In your hand that almost reached out
to touch your lover's hair, but held back instead.
Even in the index finger, as it may have tucked back
a curl before it fell around her face. In the hoofbeats
of the doe who comes unseen just after dark.

Princess Diana is Dead & Fun Town Has Closed

Everywhere at the campground, children.
Never say, *Go away & leave me in peace*,
for they do. I have brought so much baggage,

my cabin is full. Bunks where boys slept, full.
No boys begging for quarters for that last video game.
No fire-glowing marshmallows on long bent sticks.

Only ghosts—that morning I went for coffee,
my sister-in-law announcing, *Princess Diana is dead*.
We both cry. The campground cries. The world is crying.

Now, when I head out towards the highway,
I see even Fun Town has closed. Weeds overtake
mini golf course where sons shot holes-in-one.

I blink back bright sun.

Stolen Pears

—for Baron Wormser

I found myself with my neighbor at your old homestead,
your pears already half-eaten, some miraculously still hanging
from branches, skinless & chewed by squirrels, their little teeth
marks so clear. Like Eve, I reached up—any innocence left, lost.
I looked up into the Tree of Poetic Knowledge of Good & Evil,
picked the pears over as if they were for sale. Pulled the best ones
off with a *whoosh* of the leaves, a *plunk* in my bag.

But I think you'll forgive me if you know the rest of the story.
How those pears went into a cake made in memory of another poet—
a husband, a father, a farmer, an apple-grafter, a friend—
his battle with cancer lost last year. How your pears
mixed with apples from his best-loved orchard. How the spices—
like images in a poem, made the whole cake symbolic & good.
How photographs captured a pear, forgotten flowers & the long slanting roof,
stretching out in the morning sun, looking for you.

About the Author

Cynthia Brackett-Vincent is a Pushcart Prize nominee. She has published/edited *the Aurorean* poetry journal since 1995 and has had over 100 of her own poems plus nonfiction published in the United States and abroad. Her 2012 co-edited anthology, *Women on Poetry: Writing, Revising, Publishing and Teaching* (McFarland) was named one of 100 Best Books for Writers by *Poets & Writers*. Cynthia holds an AA in Social Sciences from Quincy College, a BFA in Creative Writing from the University of Maine at Farmington, and will earn an MA in English/Creative Writing—Poetry at Southern New Hampshire University in 2015. She lives in Maine with her husband and their three rescue cats where she enjoys hiking and snowshoeing. She has three grown sons, three daughters-in-law, and five grandchildren. She considers, "Grammie, what does poetry mean?" (from six-year old Noah) to be one of the best questions she has ever been asked.

Visit http://www.encirclepub.com

www.ingramcontent.com/pod-product-compliance
Lightning Source LLC
Chambersburg PA
CBHW021159080526
44588CB00008B/411